Jacob's Tree

BY HOLLY KELLER

Greenwillow Books, New York

For Corey

Watercolor paints and a black pen were were used to create the full-color art.
The text type is Futura.

Printed in Hong Kong by South China Printing Company (1988) Ltd.
First Edition 10 9 8 7 6 5 4 3 2 1

Library of Congress Cataloging-in-Publication Data

Jacob's tree / by Holly Keller.
    p.   cm.
Summary: Jacob is the smallest one in his family and although
everyone tells him he will grow, he finds it hard to wait.
ISBN 0-688-15995-8 (trade).   ISBN 0-688-15996-6 (lib. bdg.)
[1. Size—Fiction.   2. Growth—Fiction.   3. Family life—Fiction.]
I. Title   PZ.K28132Jac   1999   [E]—dc21
98-2978   CIP   AC

acob was smaller than his brother, Sidney,
smaller than his sister, Rose,
smaller than Mama,
and a lot smaller than Papa.

He was too small to reach the table.

He was too small to get a cookie from the cookie jar.

And he was too small to see himself
in the mirror over the bathroom sink.

"Wait," Mama told him.
"You'll be bigger soon."

Jacob went outside to the big elm tree.
Papa made a mark where the top of Jacob's
head touched.
"Now you will be able to see how much you grow,"
Papa said.

Jacob hated waiting.

He hated it when Sidney ran fast and he couldn't catch him.

He hated it when Rose picked apples and he couldn't reach.

And he hated it when he was the only one
who couldn't get to the top of the jungle gym.

"There's nobody to play with," he complained.

"Wait," said Mama. "And in the meantime you can play with me."

Jacob loved Mama, but he didn't want to play with her.

The leaves on the elm tree turned yellow and started to fall.

Jacob measured himself again, but he was still the same size.

"Wait," Papa said.

Jacob didn't want to wait.
He tried to make himself grow faster.

He ate a lot of vegetables because
Mama told him that would help.

He took his vitamins,

and he drank all his milk.

But when Jacob measured himself again,
he wasn't any bigger.
"Not even a little?" he asked Papa.
"Well," Papa said, "maybe a little."
Jacob knew it wasn't true.

Christmas was awful.

Grandma sent Jacob red overalls and he loved them,
but when he put them on, they were too long.

"Sidney can have them," he said.

Mama took the overalls and put them back in the box.
"Wait, Jacob," she said. "They'll fit you soon."
"I don't care," Jacob said, even though he did.

When the snow started to fall,
everything outside was white and quiet.
Inside, Mama and Papa, Sidney and Rose sat
in front of the fire.
Jacob drank hot chocolate and read his new
Christmas books.

At night he heard the wind whooshing,
and he pulled the blanket up over his head.

Days and weeks and months went by.
The branches of the elm tree hung low, and Jacob's
mark was buried in the snow.
It was too cold to go outside to play, and too snowy
for Jacob to measure himself.

One morning Jacob felt a light breeze blow
across his nose. He opened his eyes.
The sky was very blue and the snow was gone.

He went into the bathroom
to wash his face and
brush his teeth,

and he could hardly believe what he saw.
It was himself! When he looked at the mirror
over the sink, he could see his own eyes.
"Oh boy," Jacob said, and he bolted for the door.

It was true. When Papa made a mark on the tree
where the top of Jacob's head touched, it was really higher.
Jacob was so excited, he danced around the tree.

"Here," Mama said when
Jacob started to get dressed.
"Why don't you try these?"
And she gave him
the red overalls.
They fit much better.

"But they are still a little long,"
Jacob whispered to Mama.
"And what will you do?"
Mama whispered back.

"I'll WAIT!" Jacob shouted,
and he ran outside
to find Sidney and Rose.

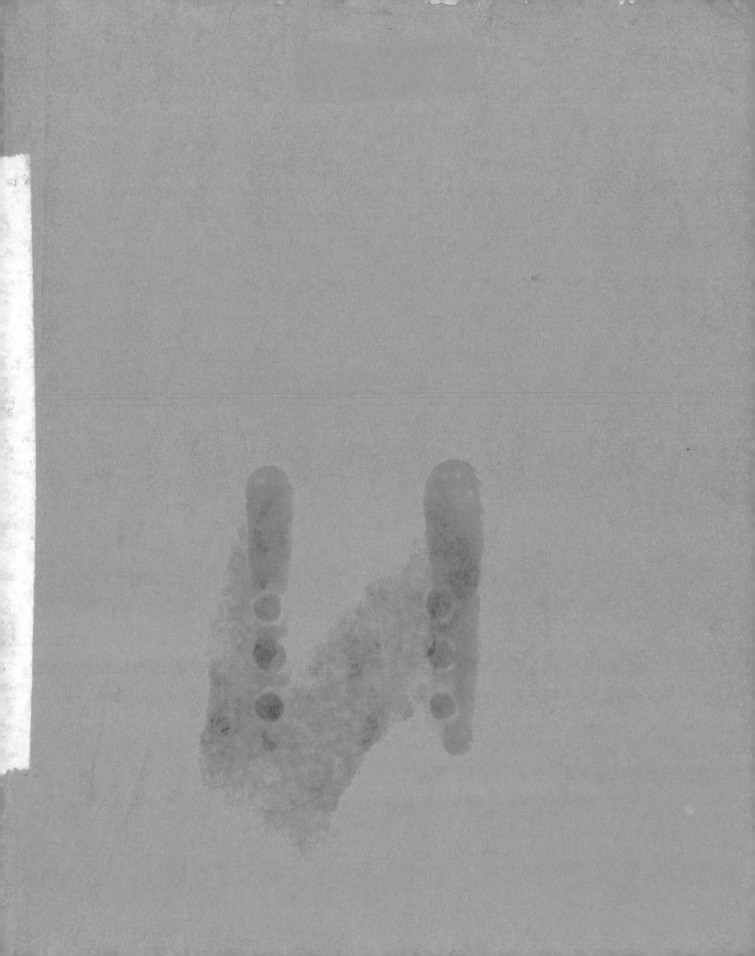

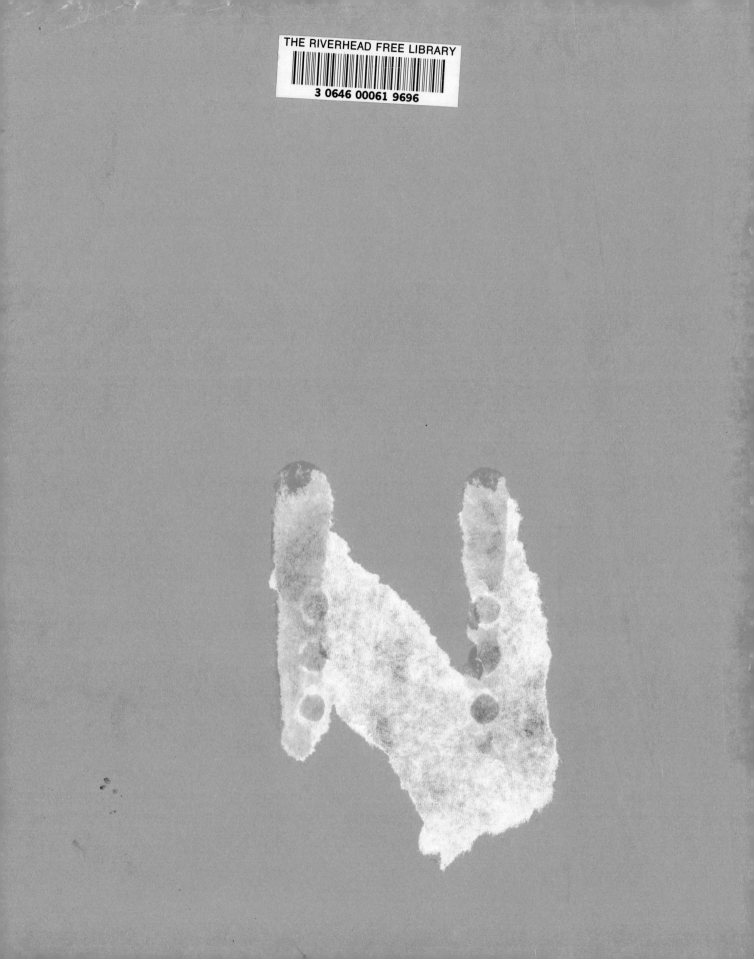